Standards

The Rough Road
to the
Common Byte

Martin C. Libicki

THE CENTER FOR ADVANCED

CONCEPTS AND TECHNOLOGY

May 1995

Center for Advanced Concepts and Technology
Institute for National Strategic Studies

NATIONAL DEFENSE UNIVERSITY

NATIONAL DEFENSE UNIVERSITY
- *President:* Lieutenant General Ervin J. Rokke, USAF
- *Vice President:* Ambassador William G. Walker

INSTITUTE FOR NATIONAL STRATEGIC STUDIES
- *Director:* Dr. Hans A. Binnendijk

DIRECTORATE OF ADVANCED CONCEPTS, TECHNOLOGIES AND INFORMATION STRATEGIES (ACTIS)
- *Director:* Dr. David S. Alberts
- Fort Lesley J. McNair, Washington, DC 20319-6000
- Phone: (202) 685-2209   ◆ Facsimile: (202) 685-3664

Opinions, conclusions, and recommendations, expressed or implied, are those of the authors. They do not necessarily reflect the views of the National Defense University, the Department of Defense, or any other U.S. Government agency. Cleared for public release; distribution unlimited.

Library of Congress Cataloging-in-Publication Data
    Standards: the Rough Road to the Common Byte
       p. cm.
    ISBN 1-55558-131-5
      1. Information technology—Standards
I. Title
T58.5 .L54
355.3'43—dc21   96-53238
                                                              CIP

First Printing, May 1995
Second Printing, March 1997

For sale by the U.S. Government Printing Office
Superintendent of Documents, Mail Stop: SSOP
Washington, DC 20402-9328 ● Phone: (202) 512-1800

ACKNOWLEDGEMENTS

The author gratefully acknowledges the very kind help of the following people, who provided information for or reviewed and commented on previous versions of this report:

Bob Akers	Stuart E. Johnson
Ray F. Albers	Carl R. Jones
Lari D. Anderson	Tom Julian
William E. Anderson	Brian Kahin
Daniel S. Appleton	Mitchell Kapor
James C. Armstrong	Philippe Kruchten
William O. Baker	William F. Lackman, Jr.
Edward R. Baldwin, Jr.	Lawrence J. Lang
James R. Bell	Michael T. Levender
Alvin H. Bernstein	Robert Leary
Joseph I. Bergmann	Robert E. Lyons
Carl Cargill	Albert R. Lubarsky
Greg Chesson	George E. Mather, Jr.
Leo Childs	Elliot Maxwell
James R. Clapper, Jr.	John S. Mayo
Fred Demech	Erik G. Mettala
Richard desJardins	Jill O. Milton
Dave Dikel	Jerry Mulvenna
David Doyle	Lee M. Paschall
Larry Druffel	Stewart D. Personick
William S. Edgerly	James Quigley
Steven P. Fried	Gordon Ray
Charles Goldfarb	Doug Schoenberger

Steven N. Goldstein
Robert T. Herres
J.B. Hilmes
Kenneth R. Jacobs
David E. Jeremiah
Theodore G. Johnson
Jerry L. Johnson

Venktesh Shukla
Yesha Y. Sivan
Casimir S. Skrzypczak
Brad Smith
Michael Spring
W.D. Wilson

These reviewers and the affiliates of the Program on Information Resources Policy at Harvard University, however, are not necessarily in agreement with the views expressed here nor should they be blamed for any errors of fact or interpretation. The views expressed are those of the author and should not be considered the views of National Defense University or the U.S. Government. Special thanks to Ellin Sarot, for editorial assistance, and to Ingrid Johnson Hotchkiss, who produced the illustrations.

This work is dedicated to my very patient wife, Denise Mazorow, and our three daughters, Ariella, Rivka, and Kayla, none of whom was yet born when this project was started.

EXECUTIVE SUMMARY

The proliferation of digital devices—each with its own way of representing and communicating information—has heightened the importance of getting these devices to talk to one another, to their applications, and to their users in mutually comprehensible tongues. Success—speaking the common byte—is prerequisite to building organizational and national and, ultimately, global information infrastructures. Failure leaves islands of connectivity, keeps systems expensive, difficult to use, and inflexible, and retards the flow of useful technology into society.

Information technology standards have been touted as a means to interoperability and software portability, but they are more easily lauded than built or followed. Users say they want low-cost, easily maintained, plug-and-play, interoperable systems, yet each user community has specific needs and few of them want to discard their existing systems. Every vendor wants to sell its own architecture and turbo-charged features, and each architecture assumes different views of a particular domain (e.g., business forms, images, databases). International standards founder on variations in culture and assumptions in North America, Europe, and Asia—for example, whether telephone companies are monopolies. Protests to the contrary, the U.S. government is a major, indeed increasingly involved, player in virtually every major standards controversy.

This paper looks at the growing but confusing body of information technology standards by concentrating on seven areas: The UNIX operating system, Open Systems Interconnection (OSI, for data communication), the Department of Defense's Continuous Acquisition and Life-cycle Support program (CALS), the Ada programming language, Integrated Services Digital Networks (ISDN, narrowband and broadband), multimedia standards (text, database, and image compression), and five specialized standards (encryption, electronic chip design, machine tools, maps, TRON). Each realm is examined from several viewpoints: the problems that need to be solved, the degree of success of standards, the role of public policy in the standards process, and major trends in each area. A subtheme throughout is the persistent divergence between the perspective of the commercial user (standards are but one possible solution to the problems of interoperability) and that of government as both customer and policymaker.

Is there a royal road to the common byte? Probably not, but history offers a few lessons: Start small, test often, leave room for growth, abjure theology, play off the dominance of the U.S., pick the layers carefully, and keep plugging.

NOTE

Under its present title, this report will be included in the published proceedings of the conference on "Standards Development and Information Structure," sponsored by the National Institute of Standards and Technology, the Science, Technology, and Public Policy Program of the Kennedy School of Government, Harvard University, and the Technology Policy Working Group, Information Infrastructure Task Force, which was held 15–16 June 1994 at Rockville, Maryland. It has also appeared as a publication of Harvard's Program on Information Resources Policy.

An extended version of this paper is being published by Butterworth–Heinemann under the title *Information Technology Standards: Quest for the Common Byte*.

TABLE OF CONTENTS

ILLUSTRATIONS

Figures

Tables

1   *What Standards Do*

Good information technology standards are common conventions for representing information as data so that finicky, but increasingly indispensable, machines may speak the common byte. Standards play a key, though poorly understood, role in the Information Era. Without them, the trillions of bytes on the Net would make little sense, intelligent machines would lose much of their brainpower, one type of equipment could not work with another, and all the data being so busily created would be accessible only to the creators.

In many ways standards are technical matters of little obvious significance; mention them and listeners' eyes glaze over. Most standards arise with little fuss, while others feature tedious Tweedledee–Tweedledum conflicts of no real import. Yet fights over the important standards matter, because the outcomes affect the architecture and politics of information. Standards require convergence on the correct question as well as the correct answer.

The fundamental issues of standards are reflected by the most basic information standard: human language. A good language has certain properties. It represents meaning efficiently and avoids unnecessary ambiguity but is robust against noise and error, ensures that a word can group like concepts, and, finally, remains alive, that is, flexible enough to absorb new meaning. Language has an architecture; it reflects and reinforces the ways by which societies construct human discourse. Thus results the extensibility of English, the logic of French, the lyricism of Italian, the fluid formality of Japanese, and the social range of Russian. Language can make particular concepts easy or difficult to convey. Life would be simpler if everyone spoke the same language, but they will not, and for good reasons.

Information technology standards exist to solve three problems. The first is interoperability, that is, getting systems to work with one another in real time (for example, telephone systems). Failure could prevent communication, but most of the time a kluge to glue systems together is sufficient. The second problem is portability, which permits software to work with heterogenous systems (for example, a consistent computer language). Again, failure could lead to closed systems, but most of the time software can be ported if more code is written to accommodate each system (or functions are dropped). The third problem is data exchange among different systems (for example, wordprocessing files). Failure could mean loss of access to information, but most of the time translators work, although with a cost in effort and dropped details. Successful standards share the ability to facilitate plug-and-play systems and induce competition among potential software and hardware providers, thus lowering costs and raising choices.

Interoperability, portability, and data exchange are usefully distinguished from one another when evaluating the need for and reach of specific standards or the consequences of their absence. Standards have costs. A convention that fits the general may be inefficient for the specific. When standards enable certain functions they inhibit others. A standard often limits efforts to extend and maintain what is standardized. The wait for standards may cause technologies to miss their markets.

All good standards go through two steps: invention and proliferation. Most are also formalized in standards bodies (sometimes prior to proliferation). Proliferation is usually more important than formalization (which is too often the focus of standards studies). De facto standards offer many of the virtues of de jure ones, particularly if the latter are a waste of time (or, worse, yet one more check-off in a government bid). But formalization has advantages: it opens the review process to outsiders (e.g., users, small vendors, and third parties), generally improves definition, and aids the inclusion of the standard in government purchases.

At the international level, communications standards come from two committees of a treaty organization, the International Telecommunications Union (ITU): the ITU-T for telecommunications and the ITU-R for radio. Computer standards come from the voluntary International Organization for Standards (ISO). NATO standards often subsume those of the United States Department of Defense (DOD).

At the national level, the American National Standards Institute (ANSI) charters committees, trade groups, and professional societies (such as the Institute of Electrical and Electronic Engineers [IEEE]) to write standards. Government standards are set by the National Institute of Standards and Technology (NIST). The DOD, the world's largest single buyer of goods and services, is influential, as is the Federal Communications Commission (FCC), the spectrum regulator.

Often proliferation is driven by strong bandwagon effects. A standard that appears to be winning will garner more support in the form of software, training, expertise, and drivers. Potential winners offer users the possibility of interacting with an increasing number of other users. Growing sales mean lower costs for conforming products. All these make the standard more appealing and lengthens its lead. Accidents of birth or early support, by starting a virtuous circle, can make a large difference in a standard's success. Can a targeted government purchase constitute sufficient early support to drive the market toward convergence on a standard? In theory, yes, but it is risky. If the market pulls away from the government (e.g., Ada, OSI), government users may be stranded. Alternatively, convergence may be forced before the embedded technology has been proved superior.

Correct comprehensiveness, timing, and family relationships influence the success of a standard. **Figure 1** shows some choices involved in choosing a standard's scope. A standard may cover only the core of a solution—that is, the functions supported by all vendors. In this case, proprietary ways of dealing with peripheral functions can frustrate interoperability for years. An overly comprehensive, perhaps anticipatory, standard, however, may cost too much to implement. By supporting alternative ways of representing essentially similar functions, such a standard can frustrate unambiguous translation between two systems. An intermediate solution is to take a large problem and divide it into layers, standardizing each. This is easier said than done, particularly if, as with data communications, standard solutions at one layer and nonstandard solutions at another do not interact well.

When should standardization occur? Premature standardization leaves no time for the market to smooth the kinks and separate out nice-to-have from need-to-have features. Late standardization yields years of market confusion and the need to cope with a proliferation of variants that arise in the interim. If the technology matures

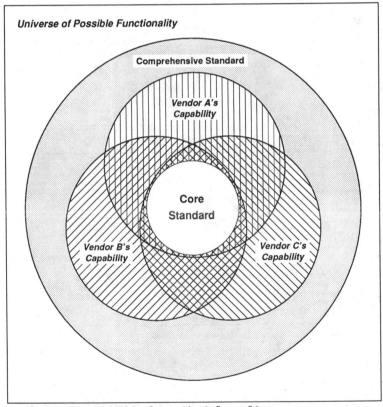

Figure 1

How Comprehensive A Standard?

before the market takes off (see **Figure 2**), standardization can occur smoothly in between. What if the market threatens to take off before the technology matures? With image compression, technology keeps getting better; a premature standard may either forestall further progress or itself be swept away by better but nonstandardized solutions.

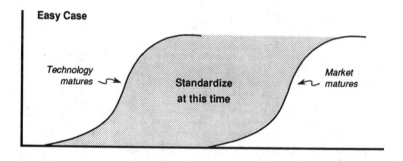

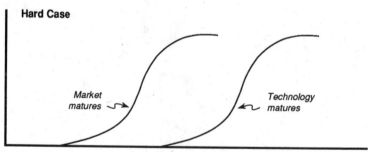

Figure 2

When Should A Technology Be Standardized?

Figure 3 shows standards clustered in families. Because a member's takeoff often carries another along, a coherent standards strategy pushes related standards. In contrast, the federal government has promoted the Ada computer language, the UNIX operating system, the OSI data communications model, and the Standard General Markup Language (SGML) text formatting system, all from competing families. Ada competes with the C computer

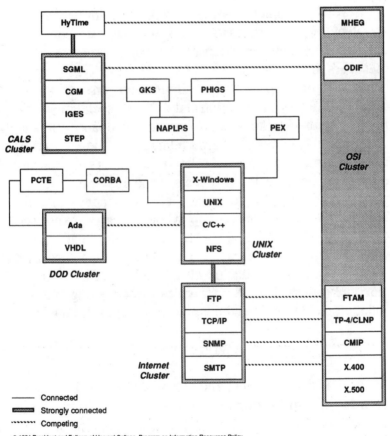

© 1994 President and Fellows of Harvard College. Program on Information Resources Policy.

Figure 3

Families of Standards

language from the UNIX family; UNIX is strongly associated with a specific transport protocol (the transmission control protocol/Internet protocol [TCP/IP]) that conflicts with OSI's, while the OSI community is associated with an open document interchange format (ODIF) that competes with SGML.

Beyond technical issues, standards influence the architecture of information. A choice of computer languages implies a relationship of programmers to their managers and to one another. Compared with a top-down communications protocol, a bottom-up one facilitates different flows of information and different social relations. Standards that make it easy to exchange and annotate computer-aided designs are related to the status of manufacturing engineers relative to that of design engineers. Because the problems standards solve are not always perceived the same way, choices among solutions influence who is connected to whom, what is expressed easily and what requires effort, whose needs matter, and who exercises influence. Standards have been touted as a way to avoid the Scilla of chaos and the Charybdis of monopoly; they shape the struggles of competing vendors and their technologies and the power of vendor versus user.

Standards also affect larger issues:

- The timing, shape, and potential of the national (and international) information infrastructure

- The internal structure of organizations (for example, from hierarchical to horizontal) and their external relationships (for example, virtual corporations)

- Choices among systems designs, from tightly integrated (which tends to be efficient) to tightly interfaced (which needs standards but is more flexible)

- The form information is likely to be seen in—linear (such as text), linked (hypertext), or lateral (database)—with further effects on the changing roles of writer and reader in providing coherence

- The speed with which new technologies come into use

- The competitiveness of the U.S. software and systems integration sector

Indeed, there are very few information issues standards do *not* affect.

Each of the seven topics presented below illustrates a theme that sets the virtues of standards against obstacles to the realization of standards. The openness of UNIX (for example, source code in public domain), for instance, has made standardization difficult. Users rejected OSI in favor of a protocol with fewer features that worked by the time they needed a standard. The DOD's Continuous Acquisition and Life-cycle Support program is impeded, because its computer-aided design (CAD) standards attempt to bridge competing paradigms of spatial information. Ada was invented for managers but rejected by programmers. The narrowband integrated services digital network (ISDN) has a known architecture and slow-to-settle standards, while broadband versions are the opposite. Multimedia standards to bring together tomorrow's digital libraries have been called for, while the requisite technologies are still jelling. Five specialized standards (encryption, electronic chip

design, machine tools, maps, and TRON) illustrate the
weakness of public standards policy in the face of market
forces.

2   *The Open Road*

Standard interfaces between layers of software—whether to run programs or to communicate data—permit the construction of systems from mix-and-match parts and free users from dominance by a single vendor. In the 1990s, all vendors pay lip service to open systems, but agreement ends there. The computer industry needs as many words for "open" as Eskimos need for snow.

Is the PC DOS architecture open? Although its well-defined software and hardware interfaces and hundred million plus user base make it a proved mix-and-match technology, one company controls the operating system and another the microprocessor. Most applications markets are dominated by a single vendor, and software struggled for years against the (640K) memory limitation that resulted from early standardization. In some respects the Macintosh, whose box and operating system come from one company, Apple, is more closed than the PC DOS system, but a well-defined user interface freed customers to switch among competing software applications without sinking time into becoming familiar with each.

Even though IBM opened its mainframe architecture by the early 1980s to allow development of plug-compatible machines, third-party peripherals, and a robust software base, many defined open as any system that would get them out from under IBM's thumb. The UNIX operating system is available from open sources but comes in so many flavors that an era of mix-and-match software is still years away. Proponents consider OSI open because it was developed in a formal process in a public forum, yet the scarcity of applications in the United States forces users to pay a premium for conforming products. To advocates of high-definition television (HDTV), open means "capable of absorbing new technology within the standard," while to the federal government, open systems mean those that can be specified in a request for proposals (RFP) without the need to mention either specific vendors or branded products.

UNIX. Open and standard, although apparently synonymous, can conflict. Openness helped UNIX spread: UNIX was the first operating system in use not exclusive to any one brand of computer (antitrust rulings kept its parent, AT&T, from selling computers). That plus the availability of its source code made UNIX popular in universities, an environment where writing and sharing code are common. When the government needed an operating system to use as a test-bed for artificial intelligence (AI) and networking, UNIX (in the version refined at Berkeley) was there to benefit. As computer scientists and engineers flowed from academia into business, they brought with them their fondness for UNIX, opening a large market for UNIX-based minicomputers and workstations. By the mid-1980s UNIX was the dominant operating system on workstations and by the end of the decade had driven most proprietary minicomputer operating systems (and many of their vendors) out of the market. UNIX is poorly suited for mainframes and microcomputers, which make up two-thirds of the market, but it dominates the remainder: supercomputers, minicomputers, and workstations.

The features that made UNIX fun to play with led to a proliferation of dialects, inhibiting the creation of a mass applications market. Personal computer users enjoy a consistent applications binary interface (ABI) that lets any software run on any machine. The absence of a dominant architecture for workstations or minicomputers (or of any successful architecturally neutral distribution format [ANDF]) limits the odds of a shrink-wrapped UNIX software market. The standardization of UNIX can, at best, foster a common applications portability interface (API), so that when source code is compiled on different machines it will act in similar ways.

Formal UNIX API standards include POSIX from an official body (IEEE) and XPG from an unofficial body (X/Open, a consortium of vendors active in Europe). XPG is more comprehensive than POSIX, but POSIX, developed in a neutral forum, has been chosen by the federal government to define UNIX. POSIX compliance, however, can be claimed by many non-UNIX systems, which allows those system to compete for government contracts when UNIX is what is really wanted.

The search for a de facto common UNIX has been a busy mating dance. Through the mid-1980s UNIX was split between versions based on AT&T UNIX and Berkeley UNIX. In 1988 AT&T united with Sun (whose co-founder helped write Berkeley UNIX) to create what was hoped would be a standard UNIX. The rest of the industry, in opposition, formed the Open Software Foundation (OSF) to develop its own version. Although the new split stalled unification, it prompted each group to compete in complementing UNIX with graphical user interfaces, network file systems, distributed computing environments, and multiprocessing architectures. In 1993, under the threat of Microsoft's Windows NT, UNIX vendors banded to support a common open systems environment (COSE).

UNIX illustrates several themes in standards:

• Standards reflect the communities they come from. UNIX's growth among small machines and within the academic environment gave it enduring characteristics: well-understood building-block function calls, cryptic names, poor documentation (UNIX users do not need user-friendly), good communications, but generally weak operational and database security.

• A respected but disinterested developer makes becoming a standard more likely. AT&T played that role for UNIX. (MIT played it for X-windows, a machine-independent graphical user interface associated with UNIX.)

• A standard does well to start small. Vendors (or their consortia) can compete to add functionality; surviving features can later be massaged into standard form.

• The openness of a technology can be inimical to standardization if vendors can tweak the source code in different ways to meet specific needs.

If Windows NT makes UNIX extinct (a prospect that seemed more likely the year before Windows NT was released), UNIX's lack of standardization will have been a contributing factor. Otherwise, even though UNIX is not standard, it still hosts most work on the cutting edge of computer technology; it is the operating system on which even microcomputer operating systems are converging.

OSI. In contrast to UNIX, which started off in a corner, OSI saw life as a comprehensive reference model for data communications that only needed to be filled in by actual standards to thrive.

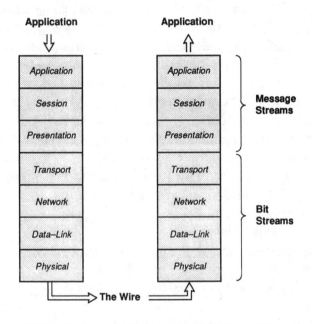

Figure 4

Open Systems Interconnection (OSI)

The OSI reference model breaks down the problem of data communication into seven layers; this division, in theory, is simple and clean, as shown in **Figure 4**. An application sends data to the *application layer*, which formats them; to the *presentation layer*, which specifies byte conversion (e.g., ASCII, byte-ordered integers); to the *session layer*, which sets up the parameters for dialogue; to the *transport layer*, which puts sequence numbers on and wraps check-sums around packets; to the *network layer*, which adds addressing and handling information; to the *data-link layer*, which adds bytes to ensure hop-to-hop integrity and media access; to the *physical layer*, which translates bits into electrical (or photonic) signals that flow out the wire. The receiver unwraps the message in reverse order, translating the signals into bits, taking the right bits off the network and retaining packets correctly addressed, ensuring message reliability and correct sequencing, establishing dialogue, reading the bytes correctly as characters, numbers, or whatever, and placing formatted bytes into the application. This wrapping and unwrapping process can be considered a flow and the successive attachment and detachment of headers. Each layer in the sender listens only to the layer above it and talks only to the one immediately below it and to a parallel layer in the receiver. It is otherwise blissfully unaware of the activities of the other layers. *If* the standards are correctly written, the services and software of any one layer can be mixed and matched with no effect on the other six.

Intent on inventing an optimal protocol, OSI's developers ended up with something not so much optimal as invented. They created standards that detail a wealth of functionality, with little market feedback on what features were worth the cost in code or machine resources. OSI standards were a long time in the making, complex with options, difficult to incorporate into products, and a burden on system resources such as memory and clock cycles.

The standards took time to fill in. The IEEE provided local area network (LAN) standards; the ITU-T supplied both the X.25 standard for public packet switching and the

X.400 electronic mail standard. The rest of the OSI standards were laboriously written during the early to mid-1980s.

Because many layers of the OSI model featured several OSI standards and because the standards were laden with options, profiles of standards (e.g., one from layer A, two from layer B) were needed to ensure interoperability within an OSI architecture. In the early 1980s General Motors sponsored a profile, the Manufacturing Applications Protocol (MAP), with a top layer that formatted instructions to automated factory equipment and two bottom layers that shuttled bits along a token bus factory LAN. Profiles were also developed for the electric utility industry and air-ground communicators. The most complete profile, shown in **Figure 5**, is the government's OSI profile (GOSIP), which became mandatory for federal purchases after August 1990.

With a reference model, standards, and profiles in hand, advocates took their show on the road—or the promise of a show; what with late standards spelling later products, they entered a world many of whose needs had been met by other standards. Most were proprietary (e.g., IBM's Systems Network Architecture [SNA], introduced in 1974). OSI's most serious competition, however, came from another open suite, the Internet's, which covered core application functions (e-mail, file transfer, remote terminals) plus transport and address mechanisms. The standards process for the Internet was completely different from that for OSI. For every new problem engineers would hack together a solution and put it out on the Internet for users to try out. If the responses were favorable, the solution was a standard.

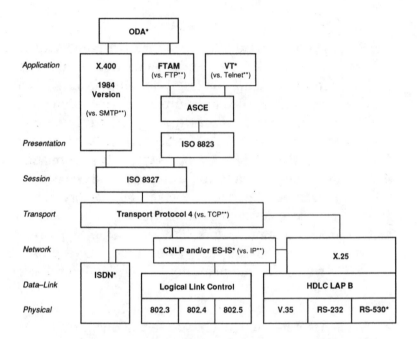

*Requirements of GOSIP 2, but not GOSIP 1. ODA, although not an ISO protocol, was included in GOSIP, because it provides services the OMB feels are required by federal agencies. Another protocol, CONS (connection-oriented network service, ISO 8878), is not shown, because it is *optional* and may be specified to link systems directly connected to X.25 WANs and ISDNs (and systems not GOSIP-compliant).

**Indicate Internet equivalents for some GOSIP standards.

Figure 5

The GOSIP 2 Stack

Thus the problem of transition strategies was born: how to build a new network protocol suite in place of, around, or between existing suites. **Figure 6** illustrates four strategies: bridging, gateway, dual-host, and encapsulation, each serving a different function.

Bridging places feature-rich OSI application layer protocols atop proven TCP/IP networks. It works by slipping in a layer of code to translate OSI's application function calls into terms the transport layer understands.

Gateways allow existing networks to communicate with other networks in a lingua franca. For every X.400 native e-mail system, for instance, there are ten X.400 gateway translators to glue other e-mail systems together.

Dual-host (more commonly, multihost) computers permit machines on heterogenous networks to use their own protocols to access a common resource (such as a supercomputer).

Encapsulation lets machines on two OSI LANs talk to each other through a TCP/IP wide area network (WAN). OSI address and transport information are treated as raw bits by the TCP/IP network, which wraps its own envelope around the data.

The four, billed as transition techniques, became in practice accommodation techniques (or general glue methods for any two protocols). OSI appears valuable primarily for its e-mail and directory standards (X.400 and X.500). Of the four strategies, bridging and gateways will probably garner the most attention.

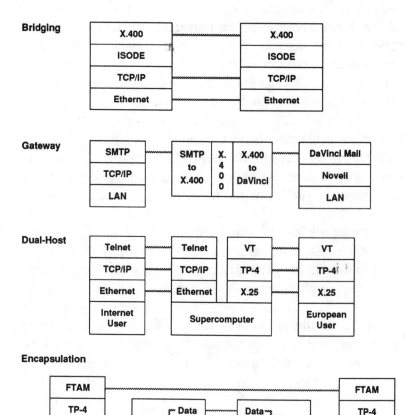

Figure 6

Infiltration Strategies

Most experts initially felt that the triumph of OSI, though slow, was inevitable. A study done in 1985 for the DOD, for instance, recommended a move to OSI not for technical reasons but because everyone else was headed there. Since about 1990 the tide has turned. Few believe OSI will do well in the U.S., and even Europe may reexamine its commitment.

What went wrong? First, contrary to theory, one size does not fit all. OSI was too heavy for personal computers and their networks but less efficient than IBM's SNA for supporting the mainframe as the data pump. OSI was left with the middle market and the glue market (sticking heterogenous platforms and networks together). The middle market went to UNIX, and thus to TCP/IP (which, for historical reasons, is free in most UNIX systems). The glue market might have gone to OSI, but when such needs surfaced in the late 1980s, OSI products were either late or too new to inspire confidence. The momentum built up by available, tested, and ready TCP/IP products and their presence on the growing Internet could not be overcome. Between 1989 and 1991 the big computer vendors, hitherto committed to OSI, backed away; by 1993 even the government was reconsidering its earlier exclusion of TCP/IP from GOSIP. The contest between rough and ready Internet standards and formally constructed OSI standards was repeated in network management (OSI's Common Management Interface Protocol [CMIP] versus the Internet's Simple Network Management Protocol [SNMP]) and path routing (OSI's Intermediate System to Intermediate System [IS-IS] protocol versus the Internet's Open Shortest Path First [OSPF] protocol), with much the same results.

Tomorrow's integrated data communications networks are likely to be a complex patchwork of proprietary protocols built around mainframes and servers (e.g., SNA and Novell's) plus Internet standards (for internetworking and systems management) and some OSI protocols (e.g., X.400 and X.500). Had the major computer companies and the government thrown their weight behind TCP/IP rather than OSI, perhaps much of the complexity might have been avoided.

3   *Front Line Manufacturing*

During the 1980s the DOD took a hard look at how information technology could promote better software and hardware, and it concluded that standards would be the core of its approach. One set of standards, CALS, was to govern the production of documentation associated with weapons systems, while another, Ada, would be the language in which defense software was written.

With standards as with any specification, the DOD always has three choices: (*i*) it can lead, by creating difficult but worthwhile challenges and supporting the search for their solution; (*ii*) it can lag, by scouting the commercial realm for good solutions and encouraging their adoption by the DOD's workers and suppliers; and (*iii*) it can mandate a separate convention that differs from what others do. The third choice is often the unintended result of seeking the first (leadership for improved interoperability) and laying claim to the second (taking standards stamped in commercial forums). Separate conventions are often worst, because they further divide the defense production base from the commercial production base. The DOD's leadership is also vitiated by mixed signals (its standards mandates compete with many more urgent internal mandates) and long development cycles (so that its standards are often out of date).

Continuous Acquisition and Life-cycle Support (CALS). The CALS initiative, begun in 1985, specifies a set of standards used in formatting text (see section **Four**) and images of technical data. CALS was intended to meet three goals. The first was to move from paper to write-once, read-many bytes. The second was to collect product data in CAD form for post-production support (i.e., recompeting, redesigning, and remanufacturing subsystems and spare parts). The third, concurrent engineering, was looked on as the most important goal. A common CAD file format would facilitate early and frequent exchange of information between prime contractors and their vendors, thereby injecting the considerations of manufacturing engineering into those of design—a way to raise quality and lower life-cycle costs.

Table 1 shows the DOD's four-level schema to represent technical imagery; each level permits increasing abstraction. Raster standards are for pictures, computer graphics metafile (CGM) for technical illustration, Initial Geometric Exchange Specification (IGES) for CAD data, and STEP for CAD/CAM (computer-aided manufacturing) data.

CALS requirements slowly seeped into contracts; the DOD's project managers wanted digital data without the expense of mandating conformance to complex standards. Only programs started since the late 1980s (thus unlikely to yield fielded systems this century) will get delivery of data in IGES form; the rest will rely on less manipulable deliverables.

The DOD had several choices in specifying how it wanted CAD data. It could have mandated delivery of all CAD data either in a format that was de facto a standard (e.g., Autocad's DXF) or one from a selected vendor (e.g., Navy's systems commands buy all CAD stations from a single vendor). It could have specified two or three formats (e.g., GM's C4 program). It could have ignored the issue and purchased format-to-format translators as needed. Instead, it chose IGES, a standard labelled as commercial but one the DOD had actually sponsored in 1979.

Table 1

CALS Standards

Standard	Purpose	IOC	Standardized
Raster	Images	Early 1990s	1980, 1984
CGM	Technical Drawings	Late 1990s	1981-1986
IGES	CAD	Early 2000s	1979-1982
STEP	CAD/CAM	Maybe never	1984-1994

IGES is generally disparaged by the DOD's customers. Although prime contractors respect the IGES mandate when dealing with the DOD, they rarely pass it down to their subcontractors, preferring to get data in the CAD format they themselves use. Failing that, translators are preferred. Only paper is less popular than IGES. IGES mandates almost never cross over from military to commercial operations of prime contractors, and IGES stands no chance of becoming any vendor's native file format.

Why has IGES done so poorly? In part because the standard was too broad and ambiguous. Internal loop tests (from a vendor's CAD format to IGES and back) drop a tenth of the data; external loop tests (one vendor's file format to another vendor's via IGES) drop a quarter. Thus, IGES requires the use of flavored CAD files—that is, files written with subsequent translation in mind. In addition, IGES files are ten times as large as native CAD files. Perhaps no neutral format could have worked. The underlying paradigm for CAD modeling is still evolving and therefore unsettled. IGES did not keep up.

Many observers, critical of IGES, aver that the Standard for the Exchange of Product (STEP) data will fix all of IGES' problems and more. At the very least, since the late 1980s the imminence of STEP inhibited the development of IGES. STEP is not just a better IGES, it is a completely new way to manage the data life-cycle of manufacturing, from design to production to maintenance. Advocates claim STEP avoids many specific mistakes of IGES and includes many general advances: built-in product conformance testing, the Express programming language (to ease building translators to CAD systems), and support for hierarchical decomposition of images. Most important, it supports object-oriented feature-based modeling. STEP represents a cement pipe differently from a shirt sleeve or a glass column, even though all are cylinders.

It would be easier to be optimistic about STEP if only it did not echo OSI. The standard has been ten years in the making but is still not a superset of IGES; its document exceeds 2,500 pages. Few products reify the technology STEP is supposed to standardize. Between the unpopularity of IGES and the vapor of STEP, it is difficult to see how CALS can promote concurrent engineering.

Since roughly 1990 the electronic delivery of technical data under CALS has been officially linked with the electronic delivery of business data under electronic data interchange (EDI). As a standard for business documents, the ANSI's X12 series has succeeded. When EDI was invented in the early 1970s, major buyers imposed their own proprietary forms, which were followed by forms developed by industry groups. The

ANSI drew the best of these together so that, as the mid-1990s near, proprietary forms are nearly gone and applications for standard forms are now submitted by groups previously disinclined to merge their forms with those of truckers and grocers. X12, however, is a domestic standard; the international standard EDI For Administration, Commerce, and Transport (EDIFACT), little used in the U.S., is slated to supersede X12 starting in 1997.

The success of X12 may be ascribed to two factors. First, X12 did not try to solve everything at once. It started with a few forms and grew. Second, the paradigms for business data (e.g., invoices) are common and mature. Electronic representation follows closely from standard business forms. In promoting EDI, the DOD (thanks to restrictive contracting law) has not been a leader but seems, to its credit, to be following in well-plowed paths.

The contrast between the success of EDI standards and the difficulties of CAD standards illustrates the greater importance of common notions over common notations in predicting a standard's success. As **Figure 7** illustrates, translation between an Ottawan's "winter" and a Quebecois "l'hiver" is easy if both refer to the same months. Similar translation between the experience of Houstonians (with their short winters) and Edmontonians (with their longer winters) is more difficult even though both use the same language.

Ada. The search for a standard computer language has been going on since the late 1950s, beginning with the development of three fundamental families. FORTRAN (formula translator) became a standard over time as the multitude of algorithms written by early users required later users to work with the language. Common Business-Oriented Language (COBOL) became a standard for business computation, in part because of federal pressure. Both Fortran and COBOL are based on old technology and have not spawned new languages in almost thirty years. Algol, an elegant language widely used only in Europe, spawned JOVIAL (an Air Force standard prior to Ada), Pascal (Ada's progenitor), and C and then C++, which in the 1990s is becoming the standard for applications development.

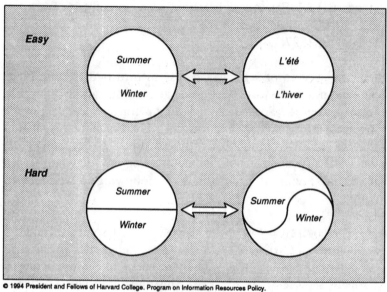

Figure 7

Translating Notations and Notions

Ada was invented when the DOD found its software costs escalating partly because it was supporting more than three hundred computer programming languages. Rather than converge on an existing language, the DOD spent the eight years from 1975 to 1983 developing one of its own. Standardization followed in lock-step order.

Any analysis of Ada must address two question: Was it a good language? Has it become a common one?

Ada was designed for the large, long-lived projects that characterize defense systems. It benefits from a solid analytical foundation and supports object-oriented design and strong type checking. But it is large, prolix, and ponderous; it produces object code that tends to run slowly and tax computer resources (although the problem is lessened with newer compilers).

Ada brought unique strengths to the realm of embedded systems. It featured exception handling (so that faults do not shut down all operations), concurrence, standard interrupt handling and protection against real-time bugs, and very high host-target portability (Ada code is often transported from development environments to weapons). The DOD hierarchy is generally satisfied with Ada's contribution to software engineering.

As a common language, the story is different. Ada's acceptance within the DOD was assured by about 1987. Many of those forced to use Ada grew to like it, and the DOD made it hard to get exceptions. Ada has also become the language of choice for non-Defense aerospace projects (e.g., the Federal Aviation Administration (FAA), the National Aeronautics and Space Administration (NASA), Boeing, Beechcraft). Outside that community it has spread poorly; advocates enumerate its users, a fact that speaks for itself.

What hurt Ada outside the DOD? Too much time was taken determining requirements, too little fieldtesting the desirability of its features. It was solidified just before object-oriented technologies caught on. Worse, Ada's model of programming was inimical to programmers. The language implicitly assumed that programmers never document code adequately, take too many short cuts, make too many sloppy errors, and look over everyone's shoulders. Managers might agree, but programmers are put off by the restrictions in the language prompted by such perceptions.

Ada's newest incarnation is Ada 95, a mere seven years in the making (1988-95). This time around managers at least recognize the need to market Ada aggressively, exploit the established vendor base, and appeal to business users. The last focus stems from efforts to make Ada a standard language for business applications within the DOD. This is a less obvious need than supporting embedded systems; standard languages already exist in these areas (such as COBOL, or MUMPS for health applications), and Ada does not hook well to database languages and user interface tools common in such environments.

Ada's fate is in doubt. Computerdom is converging on C and its object-oriented descendent, C++. In contrast to supersafe Ada, C and C++ empower the programmers, some soaring to great heights while others crash. C is what programmers learned in school (partly because UNIX programs are written in it) and so like working in after they leave.

As the emerging standard, C/C++ is the language that today's tools support, tomorrow's microprocessors are optimized for, and the global network objects of the future will be written in. Ada users, in contrast, will always be late getting new tools (e.g., computer-aided systems engineering [CASE]), new technologies (such as object-oriented programming), hooks to operating systems features (such as windows environments), and, in the thin times of the 1990s, new jobs in commercial enterprises. Ada's vendors are retreating, and the Ada mandate is being questioned more frequently at the military's highest levels.

4   *To the Gigabit Station*

The great promise of the National Information Infrastructure (NII) is the individual's ability to access all the information in the universe—data, text, image, audio, and video (both real-time and archived)—with only a computer and a telephone. The technology to realize this promise exists; its economics are not prohibitive (fiber to the home is neither necessary nor sufficient). Two types of standards are necessary for realization: those that specify how users are plugged into networks and those that format the information users receive.

As an indication of potential policy choices involved in construction of the NII, **Figure 8** illustrates capabilities that become available with increases in bandwidth, from today's analog telephones (equipped with a 14,400 bit per second [bps] modem), to dual-line ISDN phones (128,000 bps), to T1 rates (1.5 million bps), to Ethernet rates (10 million bps). Different uses require different bandwidths; even low-bandwidth digital networks (such as ISDN) enable powerful services.

ISDN. In the early 1980s the road to the gigabit station appeared obvious. Public telephone systems worldwide would install an integrated services digital network with circuits containing two 64,000 bps B lines (for voice, videotelephony, facsimile, and modems) and one 16,000 bps D line (for call-control information and packet-switched data).

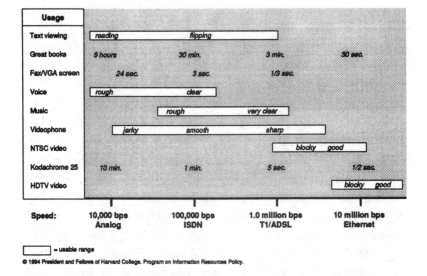

Figure 8

What Various Communications Rates Permit

ISDN could have been the second stage of the personal computer revolution. Its digital lines would have permitted major increases in data throughput. The D-channel services would have presented the nation's central office (CO) switches as just another personal computer device. The packet-switching capabilities of ISDN would have permitted remote command and control of the many smart machines that surround us. ISDN's compatibility with the nation's local loops makes it relatively inexpensive. The current cost of roughly $1,500 per connection (about $500 for each phoneset, CO-line card, and CO-switch software) could have dropped sharply had U.S. installations exceeded the present paltry rate of ten thousand a month.

As with many formal standards, ISDN took time. After a decade of discussion, in 1984 the ITU-T cobbled together enough specifications to make a standard. Implementation was to have followed quickly. In 1985 chipsets hit the market, then in 1986 ISDN-compatible CO switches, and in 1987 the first trials. On the heels of the trials surfaced the first reports of widespread incompatibilities among versions supported by the various CO vendors. The 1984 standard was too fuzzy, and, in its place, a tighter 1988 standard had to be specified. At about the same time, in 1987 Bellcore began to sponsor intensive discussions with individual switchmakers to develop compatible call control specifications. As Bellcore's ambitions were steadily pruned, in 1991 the talks resulted in the National ISDN-1 specification (demonstrated in installed switches a year later).

Yet ISDN has come to mean It Still Does Nothing. Progress remains slow, particularly in North America. Residential and small business services began only in 1992-93, and as yet there are few long-distance clear-channel lines. Corporate customers, which were expected to create initial volumes for ISDN deployment, could not wait, and they developed their own networks instead. Most D-channel services are now available on analog lines (although via a very complex user interface). Although ISDN may yet prevail in the absence of easy alternatives for user-driven digital communications devices, its success is hardly assured.

Its problems can be ascribed to two factors: mistargeted services and slow standardization. ISDN was sold on the basis of its services to very large customers (predominantly those with Centrex service), but their complex needs do not need ISDN to be satisfied. Instead, ISDN shines as a service for small and home offices, where workers rely on public infrastructure (rather than a corporate LAN). Phone companies ought to have thought of ISDN as wires and specs to link personal computers (for a fee) to the world; attic entrepreneurs of the sort that powered the personal computer revolution would do the rest.

Deliberately paced standards setting, although once appropriate for monopoly networks, was ill-suited to the far faster realm of computers. The divestiture of AT&T—erstwhile supplier of local service, long lines, switches, phonesets, and technology—deprived the standards community of its leader, whose mantle has only recently and not completely been assumed by Bellcore. The ISDN standard is extremely complex: providing B-line service was a snap; most of the difficulty was with the D-line switch-control functions (e.g., those targeted for large customers). The complexity of ISDN was also exacerbated by its goal of unifying phone systems around the world, yet ISDN calls require translations at many levels (trunk line speeds, analog-digital conversion, rate adaptation, interface levels) to cross the Atlantic.

The hoopla over the looming information highway has suggested to some that ISDN deployment might have been, at best, a brief rest stop on, and, at worst, a detour from that road. Broadband ISDN remains a mix of technologies, standards, and architectures that is far from convergent. In the early 1990s Bellcore demonstrated a technology, asymmetric digital subscriber line (ADSL), that, compared with ISDN, can transport more than ten times the bits (inbound only) on the same wires to the same distance (18,000 feet without signal regeneration) or, in its discrete multi-tone version, forty times as much to nearly the same distance (12,000 feet). Cable companies have the bandwidth to offer video-on-demand and even shared Ethernet-like services, although internal switching architectures and standard connections to long-distance services are still to be worked out.

For business communications ISDN defined the Primary Rate Interface (PRI), a 1.5 million bps service. Lacking a standard way to synchronize lines (as AT&T's Accunet does in a proprietary implementation), PRI is a bundle of 64,000 bps straws (good for PBX traffic, which has low growth rates) rather than a single pipe (which is more appropriate for data traffic, which grows far faster).

Since the mid-1980s business users have met their expanding needs for data communications by building private telephone systems from leased lines, notably T1 (at 1.5 million bps). Since 1991 quasi-public systems have been introduced to offer similar services. Two of them, frame relay and switched multimegabit data services (SMDS), were expected to take off, but their ascent has been slow, even though their standards processes, while leaving some holes, have been swift. Architectural issues plague acceptability. Frame relay is marketed as a virtual private system, and SMDS traffic is limited to single metropolitan areas. Neither frame relay nor SMDS effectively permits large data transfers outside predefined walls.

Broadband's great hope is a cell-switching technology, asynchronous transfer mode (ATM), which promises the ability to mix constant bit-rate voice, variable bit-rate video, and bursty data traffic. Its standards process has been very fast (once computer vendors perceived the LAN interconnect market and took over from the phone companies). The combination of hype (extreme even for the information industry), dozens of potential switch suppliers, the slow pace of serious interoperability testing among their switches, and the varied uses for which ATM is touted (campus LANs, private WAN interconnection, internets, telephone trunk lines, cable switching) warrant caution about its prospects.

If the NII can be defined by its services rather than by its switches, the Internet, whose standards became its architecture, has succeeded as a model by any measure. It reaches twenty million people on two million hosts in more than a hundred countries. To become the global information infrastructure, the Internet will need to overcome two deficiencies. First, its orientation to packet switching (coupled with nontrivial message delays and heterogeneous access rates) inhibits its support of real-time voice and video. Second, a system built to support subsidized academic and government uses is having difficulty coping with growth. New standards need to be created to expand its address space, enlarge its routing tables, and separate paying customers from free riders. To complete the circle, as Internet access becomes widely available to users outside institutions, it may drive a demand for ISDN-type access speeds and thus propel the ISDN along.

Narrowband ISDN had a settled architecture, but its standards were too long getting settled. The broadband version seems to have standardized faster, but its architecture remains in flux. Time—and success—will tell which, stable standards or settled architecture, matters more.

The Congress of Libraries. The standards that would organize the formatting, accessing, and compression of information within tomorrow's congress of libraries are in various states of repair; many are attempting to coalesce before the technology behind them has settled.

One problem is how to go past ASCII's standard for text in order to represent documents that also contain metatext (e.g., italics), hypertext (even footnotes), and images. Two approaches are possible. The first represents layout and other metatext directly; the second specifies a grammar to separate text and metatext (to be processed separately).

The DOD's CALS program selected the second approach, in the form of SGML, a standard way to define and mark nontext features. SGML technology has advantages for CALS beyond ensuring a consistent organization (and look) for DOD manuals and other publications. Formatted documents are essentially free-form databases; a marked-up document can be sliced and diced into a variety of reports. SGML also lends itself to hypertext, which many consider the best electronic expression of a maintenance manual.

By removing formatting decisions from authors, SGML supports many-to-one publishing well, but it supports peer-to-peer exchange of documents poorly. Because it is a metastandard, two systems must support a standard tag set to interchange documents. The DOD has an official tag set for technical manuals; book publishers, classicists, and airlines, among others, each have their own. All of these are different and not interoperable. Such differences may not matter initially (few classicists read tank repair manuals), but interdomain exchange and software portability require a convergence of tag sets, something less likely with every new set invented. Documents must contain (or reference) not only the material itself but also the tag set and the output specifier (to convert mark-up into page-printing instructions) before they can be exchanged.

Widespread adoption of SGML, by making one cluster of functions easier, inhibits the rise of alternative standards to facilitate other clusters. A standard extended ASCII for metatext is likely to be preempted by Unicode, a 16 bit extension to represent every language's alphabets. Other methods of direct format representation include Microsoft's Rich Text Format (which primarily supports fonts), Adobe's Postscript page-description language, and its successor, the Portable Document Format. The last may achieve de facto status for representing pages (as unrevisable images), but its use requires purchasing Adobe's software. In the absence of a common format, direct translation among popular wordprocessing formats leaves much to be desired.

Query systems for the digital congress of libraries—or, at least, the fraction kept as databases—have been successfully standardized. Following the invention of the relational database in 1969, IBM released the specifications for its structured query language (SQL) in 1976, which it commercialized for mainframes in the early 1980s. Because IBM boxes ruled the corporate data warehouse, every other major vendor of database management software felt required to follow suit and support SQL, which they did between 1985 and 1988.

Like UNIX, SQL has continued to evolve with deeper and richer colors. In 1986, SQL received ANSI imprimatur, with subsequent versions appearing in 1989 and 1992. Each successive version is more complex—sometimes following and sometimes inducing corresponding features in products. Again like UNIX, the portability of SQL, never perfect, continues to improve for the core functions, as other functions, less well standardized, are added. In 1989, the SQL Access Group was formed to tighten the standard (X/Open and NIST, too, worked on the issue). The group also sought to promote SQL's companion in interoperability, remote database access (RDA), so that clients using one database management system could access data managed by another.

Image compression is necessary for the digital library, because the picture worth a thousands words needs fifty thousand words' worth of bytes to be transmitted. Technology permits lossless compression at ratios of 10:1, acceptable lossy compression at 30:1, and workable compression at higher rates. A surfeit, not a lack, of standards is the problem. Fax machines support two standards; videophones, one; still and motion pictures one each; television, several; and the list does not include either de facto standards or efficient but unstandardized approaches.

For real-time videophone compression, the ITU-S's H.261 standard provides least-common-denominator interoperability. Every major vendor of encoder-decoder (codec) boxes claims its proprietary algorithms can support twice the data rate H.261 does at the same level of quality. They will keep the videoconferencing market, while H.261 is expected to prevail on personal computer-based systems (where clarity is less an issue because video windows are smaller than full screen).

Official standards for still and motion picture image compression (JPEG and MPEG, respectively) are gathering support. Yet, newer technologies, wavelet and fractal compression schemes (both funded by the DOD's Advanced Research Projects Agency [ARPA]), are frequently better (because they produce less objectionable artifacts at high rates of compression). Other schemes, such as Intel's Indeo and Media Vision's Captain Crunch, are less efficient but work without a dedicated hardware chip. Standardization before the technology was fully developed may be premature.

The search for a television compression standard was buffeted by two unexpected developments. The FCC's 1989 dictate that HDTV signals must fit within the narrow spectrum now allocated for analog television effectively ended the front runner status of Japan's MUSE analog technology in favor of a digitally compressed signal. In 1992, aggressive cable companies announced they could use compression to offer five hundred channels (mostly for video on demand) along existing coaxial wiring. In contrast to terrestrial service, which uses many broadcasters (each of them necessarily using the same standard), neighborhoods tend to be served by a single provider that can impose a compression format on its subscriber base. Standards are not necessary, although they can keep costs down.

5   *Lessons and Prognostications*

The search for better standards (or better paths to what standards provide) continues. The quest can be summarized by looking at five areas that illustrate the limits of government standards policy, exploring a future for standards, and drawing some lessons.

Limits of Standards Policy. Although in theory public policy can promote growth in particular sectors by adroit backing of standards, in practice its influence is circumscribed. For example:

• As the major buyer and developer of encryption and digital-signature technology, the federal government can be expected to be a large influence on creating standards, but public policy has not resolved the tension between the government's desire to support commercial security and its desire to tap into private and foreign data streams. Thus, the government's standards efforts are increasingly suspect.

• The DOD financed an electronic CAD standard, the very-high-speed integrated circuit (VHSIC) hardware description language (VHDL), and mandated it for a certain class of chips, but the standard did not catch on. Unexpectedly, however, a private firm, Cadence, boosted its own proprietary language, Verilog, to de facto status. Cadence's competitors, in response, rallied around VHDL, available as a de jure standard, which then took off.

● The DOD has also supported development of a standard for machine tool controllers, in part to support machine tool builders competing with Japan, which had a single controller vendor. U.S. companies earlier unable to unite on a de facto standard, however, appear unable to unite on one supported by the DOD.

● As the world's largest collector and archiver of map data, the U.S. government ought to be able to set standards for its archived data and, by so doing, influence how everyone represents map data. The government's spatial data transfer standard (SDTS) was a trifle too long in the making. In the early 1990s private repackagers of geographical data began to use incompatible approaches based on older formats.

● Japan tried to counter U.S. dominance in microprocessors and operating systems by having electronic firms adopt a single standard, The Real-time Operating Nucleus (TRON). But a standard by itself appears unable to help Japanese producers in this area.

The Future of Standards. If microcomputer markets are any indication, the conflict between closed and open architectures may be settled by the rise of owned architectures (see **Figure 9**). In a closed architecture (e.g., IBM or AT&T circa 1975) a single vendor defines and sells most of the basic systems on one side of the interface and the software on the other side. In an open architecture, the interfaces are externally defined, often in open forums, and vendors compete in the segments delineated by the interfaces. In an owned architecture, a single vendor sells all or most of a segment and by its dominance establishes an interface whose specifications are released to the public. Other vendors develop products that support that interface, and thus the interface becomes entrenched as the de facto standard. The architect nevertheless retains control, either by owning the technology needed to make the interface work (e.g., Adobe) or by using a deep knowledge of the interface to stay a generation ahead of rivals (e.g., Intel).

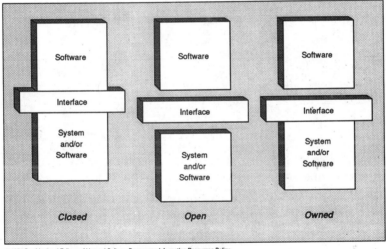

Figure 9

Closed, Open, and Owned Architectures

Sometimes the architect profits solely through its market clout in the basic segment (e.g., Hewlett–Packard in laser printers). Occasionally a vendor that dominates one segment uses knowledge of the interface to dominate another. Microsoft's knowledge of its Windows environment, for instance, allowed it to jump off to an early (and perhaps sustainable) lead in Windows-compatible applications software. In contrast, its knowledge of DOS provided no such advantage.

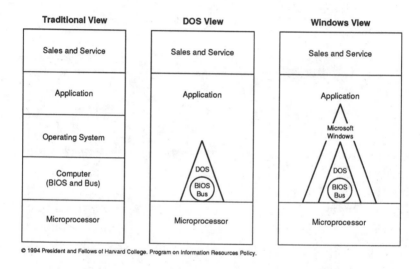

Figure 10

Altering the Interfaces of the Microcomputer World

Figure 10 suggests why Windows had a greater effect. Computer markets are typically shown as segmented by one-dimensional interfaces. The interface between DOS and an application tends to be short, that is, information-poor; applications write directly to the chip. The interface between Windows and typical applications is long, that is, information-rich (the applications make many calls on Windows functions). If Microsoft's object-linking and embedding technology proves functional and popular, the interface will be richer yet. The richer the interface, the more difficult to master and thus more important to control. Other vendors compete with owners of dominant interfaces, not by breaking into the original operating systems or groupware— that establish alternative interfaces as more important architecture but by developing new uses—such as network operating systems or groupware — that establish alternative interfaces as more important.

How useful is the layer model for comprehending standards? The OSI's travails should have suggested that layers may be misleading. Perhaps software should be understood as clusters of objects—packages that combine data-structures, data, and operations defined on the data. Such packaging provides well defined but extensible interfaces. Accessing these objects requires both standard ways to call them and standard ways to package them so they behave predictably. To this end, a consortium, the Object Management Group (OMG), developed a common object-request broker architecture (CORBA), which enjoys wide support but needs far more definition to be truly useful.

Powering the challenge of integration is the increasing convergence of the entire information industry. The personal computer model of a lone user on a stand-alone machine running a single application is giving way to networked groups running applications that must work with one another (**Figure 11** shows a typical profile). The scale of integration is rising from the user to the office, the institution, and sooner, rather than later, the universe.

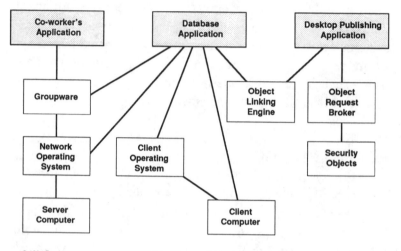

Figure 11

Objects Rather than Layers

With increases in scale comes a shift in the purposes of standardization, as **Figure 12** shows. For the lone user standards provided familiarity with systems built from plug-and-play components made cheap through competition among clones. For the institution familiarity matters less and interoperability more; standards help users knit heterogenous legacy systems into a functioning whole. At the global level plug-and-play declines in importance, while political issues of architecture influenced by competing standards assume importance.

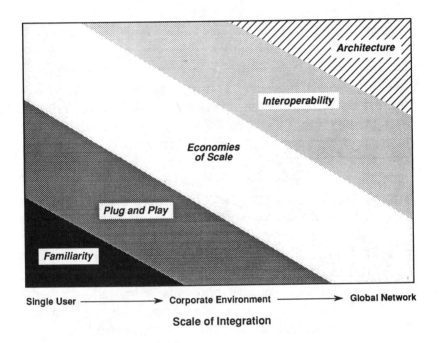

Scale of Integration

Figure 12

**The Growth in the Scale of Integration
Changes What Standards are Good For**

Interoperability is often understood as a way of making two parallel systems (e.g., workstations on two networks) talk to each other. Yet conversion or translation is always possible with enough work; what matters is how much. Rival products, each attempting to own an architecture, cover territory differently, and gluing them to create, say, an open database architecture may require varied methods: front-end APIs; gateways, structured and open; SQL routing; and database encapsulation. Each method emphasizes another standard, some more formal than others. The OSF melds suites in many ways at once—by incorporation, extension, hooks above, hooks below, and, if all else fails, by gateways and translation. Parts of this can always talk to parts of that, but which parts varies by case. Putting virtual layers (e.g., hardware abstraction layers) above real ones is another way standards can glue systems together. CASE, as another example, is looked to as a way to surmount problems caused by multiple computer languages, but its tools must be inter-operable—calling for yet more standards (e.g., the portable common tools environment [PCTE] from Europe).

Standards become critical for the external systems integration necessary to building tomorrow's networks, which will unite users, instruments, sensors, and software with contributions from governments, corporations, and other institutions. One network might monitor the earth's environment, trading data and rules back and forth; another may do the same for personal health, linking medical sensors with monitoring stations, expert systems, and doctors. Microstandards are needed to ensure that data (the nouns and adjectives) are defined in mutually comprehensible ways while functions (the verbs) can interact predictably.

So Many Standards, So Little Time. The worth of or rationales for information technology standards are empirical: Do conventions work? Are they common? Are they sufficient to meld heterogenous applications, products, and systems smoothly?

For those who cannot tell the standards without a scorecard, **Tables 2–4** summarize standards in three ways: their status as common conventions, their origins and spread, and the influence of standards groups and the government on their development. Forty-one standards are classified according to whether they promote interoperability, portability, or data exchange, an imprecise trichotomy (many interoperability standards, for instance, promote software portability and data exchange).

Table 2 places standards in one of eight groups (largely on the basis of how they fare in North America). *Winners* are well accepted conventions subdivided into *stable winners*, *unstable winners* (which may be overtaken, particularly by microcomputer conventions), and *chaotic winners* (which may spawn multiple versions at higher speeds). *Niche* standards are stable within a well-defined segment but failed to penetrate the entire market; some (e.g., Ada, ISDN, CMIP) may, for that reason, be considered *losers*. *Comers* are not well accepted but seem to be growing toward that status. *Babies* have yet to emerge strongly into the market; they are divided into *healthy* and *sick* on the basis of their prospects. *Losers* are self-explanatory.

The volatility of information technology, and thus, supposedly, its standards, may call such judgements into question, yet the stability of the fate of these standards over the two years since initial assessments were made is remarkable. The few shifts worth noting include:

- De facto microcomputer standards may put winners from the UNIX cluster at risk.

- Two CALS standards, CGM and SGML, are becoming popular more quickly than seemed likely earlier. An implementation of SGML, the Hypertext

Markup Language (HTML), has become a *de facto* standard with the Worldwide Web.

Table 2

The Status of Specific Standards

	Interoperability	Portability	Data Exchange
Stable Winners	SNMP, Group 3 Fax, SS7, Fanuc Controllers	BIOS/DOS, SQL, VHDL	Postscript, TIFF, HTML
Unstable Winners	TCP/IP, X-Windows	UNIX	EDI X12
Chaotic Winners	802 LANs, Modems		
Niche	CMIP, MUSE, Z39.50, X.400, X.500, ISDN	Ada	Group 4 Fax, DES/DSS, EDIFACT
Comers	H.261		SGML, CGM, SDTS, JPEG, MPEG
Healthy Babies	FCC-HDTV, ATM, Frame Relay		
Sick Babies	NGC, SMDS	PCTE	STEP
Losers	OSI Organic	TRON	IGES

● Official compression standards are facing a tougher fight from software-based methodologies and new technologies

● ATM may eclipse the emergence of frame relay and SMDS

Table 3

Source and Spread of Standards

	Inter-operability	Portability	Data Exchange
U.S. Origin, Not Exported	SNMP, NGC, TCP/IP, FCC-HDTV, Frame Relay		EDI X12, HyTime, IGES, SDTS DES/DSS
U.S. Origin, Exported	X-Windows, Modem, Z39.50, 802 LAN, SMDS	UNIX, Ada, SQL, VHDL, CORBA BIOS/DOS	SGML, HTML, TIFF, Postscript
Global	CMIP, SS7, H.261, OSI Organic, X.400/X.500, ATM, ISDN	PCTE	STEP, CGM, EDIFACT, JPEG, MPEG
Japan	Group 3 Fax, Fanuc Controller, MUSE	TRON	Group 4 Fax

Table 3 sorts standards by origin and spread. Of the forty-one listed, twenty-four originated in the U.S. (broadly defined to include U.S.-based multinationals, imports such as Ada in response to U.S.-generated requirements, foreign nationals based in the U.S., and the now global Internet community). Although many of these forty-one are used overseas, ten are confined mainly to North America. Another twelve (eight from ITU) are considered global in origin, with strong U.S. input. Of the five distinctly Japanese in origin, two are unlikely to see much use outside Japan. As a rough generalization, the U.S. originates perhaps two-thirds of all software and the same share of its standards. The U.S. chairs only one-fifth of the ISO's computer subcommittees, however, and has only one vote in the ITU.

The search for the one true standard and the process of formal standardization are not the same (see **Figure 13**). Consensus standards may be unnecessary in some situations; where they are needed, informal arrangements may suffice. The Internet and X/Open produce workable and robust standards, and vendor consortia (such as the ATM Forum) have proved capable of filling gaps and tightening loose ends left by more formal efforts. Conversely, some formal efforts result in competing standards (e.g., SGML versus ODIF) or standards that need considerable refinement to be useful.

To supply a de facto standard a vendor does not need to be the industry gorilla. The influence of IBM on some standards has varied greatly: from positive (SQL, DOS/BIOS PCs), to neutral (its Extended Binary Coded Decimal Inter-Change [EBCDIC] alternative to ASCII, its Distributed RDA), to counter-positive (OSI and UNIX were favored to limit IBM's dominance). Will Microsoft, often viewed as IBM's successor, be more successful? User-written standards (e.g., Ada, MAP) are not necessarily winners either.

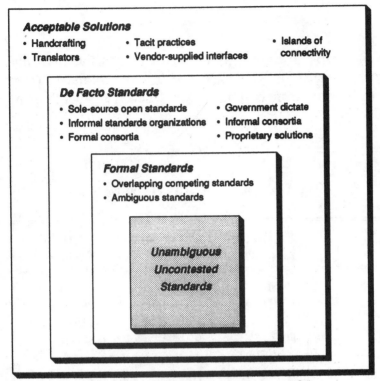

Acceptable Solutions
- Handcrafting
- Translators
- Tacit practices
- Vendor-supplied interfaces
- Islands of connectivity

De Facto Standards
- Sole-source open standards
- Informal standards organizations
- Formal consortia
- Government dictate
- Informal consortia
- Proprietary solutions

Formal Standards
- Overlapping competing standards
- Ambiguous standards

Unambiguous Uncontested Standards

© 1994 President and Fellows of Harvard College. Program on Information Resources Policy.

Figure 13

Standards and Standardization

Table 4 presents standards in five categories according to the importance of formalization to their spread. *Nil* means that formal standards bodies have yet to play: personal computer standards, Internet-based standards, and those where government efforts are ongoing. For five standards, formalization came *after the fact*, that is, after development, and affected spread only modestly. F i v e were developed outside standards bodies and taken inside for *imprimatur*, which then became critical to their credibility. The rest, labelled *critical*, were deliberately and specifically developed in standards bodies and are mostly interoperability standards. The U.S. government has played a major role in almost half of the forty-one standards. Nine were created by government policy or program. Three others were strongly supported by GOSIP, another three by CALS.

Table 4

The Role of Standards Organizations

	Inter-operability	Portability	Data Exchange
Nil	SNMP, NGC*, X-Windows, TCP/IP*, FCC-HDTV*, SMDS, Fanuc Controller	BIOS/DOS, TRON°, CORBA	DES/DSS*, Postscript, TIFF, SDTS*, HMTL
After-the-Fact		UNIX°, Ada*, SQL, VHDL*	SGML°
Impri-matur	Group 3 Fax, Z39.50*, 802 LANs, MUSE		IGES*, Group 4 Fax
Essential	CMIP°, SS7, Modem, H.261, X.400/X.500, ATM, Frame Relay, ISDN, OSI Organic	PCTE°	EDI X12, HyTime, STEP°, CGM°, EDIFACT, JPEG, MPEG

*   Sponsored by U.S. Government

° Other U.S. Government Involvement

In spite of so much government activity, public policy does not merit high marks. NIST's emphasis on open systems, software portability, and vendor independence accurately and wisely presaged the market, but execution has been less stellar: GOSIP did little good, POSIX was a poor vehicle for UNIX standardization, and NIST lost credibility in cryptology controversies. The emphasis of the DOD on the portability of software and documentation was wise, although the uniqueness of the Department's problems are often unrecognized. The DOD to its credit has promoted TCP/IP, SGML, and CGM, but IGES is universally disparaged and the failure of Ada to win support outside aerospace (while otherwise a good language) has left its users out on a technological limb. The free market shibboleths of the FCC prevented the emergence of AM stereo and left ISDN without support, but its mandate that HDTV must fit into existing bandwidths spurred image compression. The government, lacking the heavy handedness of its European counterparts, has at least let the native U.S. genius at software proceed unimpeded.

So why has public policy not been better? First, because government is ponderous; it gets under way slowly and once a course is set plods on, well after everyone else may have taken a different path. Second, because federal policy has an inordinate respect for international standards bodies, even though the U.S. is underrepresented in them. Third, because public policy often responds to the peculiar needs of users in the government in general (such as vendor neutrality) or in the DOD in particular (such as the need to support large, centralized projects). Federal standards policy is inescapably an aspect of economic strategy: deliberate choices are made (passing the buck to an international organization is still a choice) whose success would create winners and losers and has ramifications for the entire economy (as proponents might wish, even though such efforts are technically oriented to government users only).

If the rough road to the common byte teaches anything, it is that successful standards start small and grow with consensus on the core. The linked standards of UNIX, the C programming language, and TCP/IP all started as simple, elegant solutions to problems that grew to meet increasingly complex needs; HTML, SQL and X12 started life much smaller than they stand today.

The OSI edifice, in contrast, is large, complex, and notoriously unsuccessful in North America; the parts that did well—X.25 and X.400—were not written by the ISO. ISDN has been similarly retarded by its bulk. Standards are risky if they are based on technologies that have not been tested in working products accepted by the market. Ada is a prime example of specifications preceding realization.

Although any specific approach to standards must be sensitive to particulars of the relevant technology, applications, and markets, the one emerging from the standards community reflects these lessons: collect a small group of vendors, write a small, simple specification that covers the important functions, omit nonessentials, leave room for both new technologies and possible backtracking, identify real-world test-beds for the standard, and get it out the door as soon as possible. This approach suggests government standards policy concentrate on the following questions:

- What problem is standardization needed to solve?

- Must the problem be solved through collective means; must it be solved internationally?

- What is the smallest solution, and can it be broken into manageable chunks?

- What are the best tools (e.g., imprimatur, research and development, targeted purchases, regulation) to promote convergence that also permit backing off if they fail?

- Should a domestic solution be exported?

Are standards ultimately irrelevant? Given enough time, faster hardware and smarter software will, if not end the standards problem, reduce it to very low levels of discomfort. Yet the architecture of information that today's standards permit will persist, because the social relationships they create reinforce themselves. Decisions on who can say what to whom about what have both explicit and implicit dimensions, and standards play a powerful role in the implicit ones. Getting the architecture right is what matters; standards policy then accommodates it, not the other way around. The vision of the international information infrastructure should persist; the communion of bytes should follow.

Acronyms

ABI	applications binary interface
ADSL	asymmetric digital subscriber line
AI	artificial intelligence
ANDF	architecturally neutral distribution format
ANSI	American National Standards Institute
API	applications portability interface
ARPA	Advanced Research Projects Agency (under the DOD)
ASCII	American Standard Code for Information Interchange
ATM	asynchronous transfer mode
BIOS	basic input-output system
BPS	bits per second
CAD	computer-aided design
CALS	Continuous Acquisition and Life-Cycle Support
CAM	computer-aided manufacturing
CASE	computer-aided systems engineering
CGM	computer graphics metafile
CMIP	Common Management Information Protocol
CO	central office
COBOL	COmmon Business-Oriented Language
CODEC	encoder-decoder
CORBA	common object-request broker architecture
COSE	common open systems environment
DOD	Department of Defense
DOS	disk operating system
DXF	Digital Exchange Format

EBCDIC   Extended Binary Coded Decimal
           Inter-Change
EDI   electronic data interchange
EDIFACT   EDI for Administration, Commerce, and
           Transport

FAA   Federal Aviation Administration
FCC   Federal Communications Commission
FIPS   federal information-processing standards
FORTRAN   Formula Translator

GOSIP   Government Open Systems Interconnection
           Protocol

HDTV   high-definition television
HTML   Hypertext Markup Language

IGES   Initial Geometric Exchange Specification
IOC   initial operational capability
IS-IS   intermediate system–intermediate system
ISDN   integrated systems digital network
ISO   International Organization for Standards
ITU   International Telecommunications Union
ITU-R   ITU, radio standards subcommittee
ITU-T   ITU, telecommunications standards
           subcommittee

JOVIAL   Jules' Own Version of International
           Algebraic Language
JPEG   Joint Photographics Experts Group

LAN   local area network

MAP   Manufacturing Applications Protocol
MPEG   Motion Picture Experts Group

MUMPS	Massachusetts's General Hospital Utility Multi-Programming System
MUSE	MUltiple Sub-Nyquist Encoding
NASA	National Aeronautics and Space Administration
NATO	North Atlantic Treaty Organization
NII	National Information Infrastructure
NIST	National Institute of Standards and Technology
ODIF	Open Document Interchange Format
OMG	Object Management Group
OSF	Open Software Foundation
OSPF	Open Shortest Path First
PBX	private branch exchange
PCTE	portable common tools environment
POSIX	Portable Open Systems Interface for computer environments
PRI	primary rate interface
RDA	remote database access
RFP	request for proposals
SDTS	spatial data transfer standard
SGML	Standard General Markup Language
SMDS	switched multimegabit data services
SNA	Systems Network Architecture
SNMP	Simple Network Management Protocol
SQL	Structured Query Language
STEP	Standard for the Exchange of Product
TCP/IP	transmission control protocol/Internet protocol

TRON	The Real-time Operating Nucleus
VHDL	VHSIC hardware description language
VHSIC	very high-speed integrated circuit

WAN	wide area network

XPG	X/Open Portability Guide

*U.S. G.P.O:1997-418-295:60010